The Rampaging Saffron

Arun Murugesan

notionpress
.com

INDIA · SINGAPORE · MALAYSIA

Notion Press

Old No. 38, New No. 6
McNichols Road, Chetpet
Chennai - 600 031

First Published by Notion Press 2019
Copyright © Arun Murugesan 2019
All Rights Reserved.

ISBN 978-1-64587-876-6

Dedicated as a short summary to all Indians who have assiduously sworn to be secular, tolerant and liberal despite the scourge of hate and divisive politics that is fast engulfing India.

India is staring at uncertainty, in about 70 years since independence, the foundation on which the envious idea called INDIA was built- a pot- pourri of different cultures, peoples & plurality being the standard, has become shaky. Indians are staring at each other and looking differently- the dangerous spectre of identity politics is mushrooming to emerge as a major threat to the unity and integrity of India. The Sangh Parivar spear headed by RSS has been active in pre & post Independent India, but without political power for quite a while, which is now vested with its protégé the Bharatiya Janata Party. They were only on the side lines for a very long time but made sure that they had a disciplined cadre who were dedicated to their rabid and communal ideology.

Ever since the BJP came to power riding on the popular slogans of "SABA KA SAATH SAB KA VIKAS" & "ACHHE DIN" in 2014, the narratives that defined India are being dismantled in a systematic manner in full public view. The young and aspirational India which was fully disillusioned with the UPA government's scam-ridden tenure, gave a huge thumbs up to the BJP regime- that took over from them. With the 5 year term over, it is really not known as to how many of these people have seen through the game plan of the Sangh Parivar. If these educated Indians for whom corruption was a big thorn in the flesh, also realize that disruption of the social environment which comprises of a diverse population, co-existing for decades is also a bigger problem then the change for the better in terms of the political landscape is in the offing.

The term secularism has become so common place that many politicians misinterpret it in a different manner and send home a wrong signal to the people. The Sangh Parivar has tampered with the meaning in so many different ways, that many of the Indians do not really understand the true essence of secularism. Secular means **not religious or spiritual**. When Dr. Ambedkar framed the Constitution of India in 1950, he coined the term Secular Democratic Republic of India. The term simply denoted that religion shall strictly be kept away from politics, as in the West where the church never interfered with the state. The Grand old party the Congress which has ruled the country for most of the 70 years-has thrived in the absence of a strong secular opposition party & has always dilly-dallied on the concept of secularism & has changed stance many a times to suit its selfish interests.

The opposition as an alternative to Congress has been the BJP under the umbrella of the Sangh Parivar & without doubt conforms to the right wing ideology with a majoritarian mindset. It is amazing as to how a party that had just 2 seats in the LOK SABHA in the year 1989, has become such a potent force in 2019, spreading its tentacles far & wide in the country presenting a lurking and imminent danger to the integrity of the country. It is evident that as per the founding principles of the nation & even as per the norms laid out by the Election commission of India for political parties, the BJP cannot have found its space in the political arena but for the lackadaisical attitude of government institutions.

It is clear that the Sangh Parivar is keen to implement its hidden agenda under the so called garb of development. The term secularism shot to fame when a veteran BJP leader phrased, the term pseudo-secular for Congress & other Left parties who according to him were pampering the minorities especially the Muslims at the expense of the majority Hindus. The hardliner infact catapulted the party to centre stage by his series of hate speeches, jostled in his rath which undertook the yatra-North to South, East to West & thereby creating communal frenzy & hundreds of deaths in communal riots as an aftermath. The hardcore Sangh Parivar workers poisoned the Indian minds into believing that secularism meant that every Indian should be treated as equal irrespective of his religious affiliation & this provided easy fodder for gullible minds.

The veteran BJP leader is also famous for formulating the word minority appeasement which still continues to be a popular idiom for the Sangh Parivar to attack its opposition especially the Congress. The term implied that the minorities especially the Muslims are being appeased denying the same set of privileges to the majority community- the Hindus. It is really shocking to see how disturbing narratives are built on a false premise, as is this case. In a country where the majority Hindus dominate every sphere of activity of business from Gujarat to Bengal & from Punjab to Tamil Nadu, one cannot really find out a single trade or activity where the Muslims have dominated the majority by being appeased unfairly by the so called secular parties, as annotated by the saffron brigade. In short secularism can never be a part of the Sangh Parivar's vocabulary or dictionary for that matter, unfortunately though their so called interpretation of this word, is firmly ensconced in the minds of Young India. The founders of modern India had visualized a political class which firmly believed in a liberal society, was egalitarian & everybody believed in harmony, never did they advocate a concept where religion is mixed freely with politics & is responsible for generation of a dangerous cocktail of hate politics.

Even if the Sangh Parivar which is championing the cause of the majority & who it believes are discriminated against by pseudo-secularists, libtards - the various names as propounded by their belligerent affiliates, is of the assumption that we are a Hindu majority state & Hinduism should be the way of life then the whole idea should be put to a referendum to the people of India. It is presumed that the return to primitive mindset shall have no impact on the generous dose of idea of (NEW INDIA) loudly echoed by the BJP government. In a democracy, the people represent the heart of the nation & they continue to be the best judges to decide on what could be apt & representative for the nation in today's context. The politicians should simply not believe that both houses of parliament are empowered to decide on such matters of great national importance. The Sangh Parivar shall not dare to undertake this exercise since the diversity of this country will make it impossible for the task of this nature to be implemented and is bound to be arduous in the long run.

Even if the right wing elements excitedly indulge in this adventurism-they are sure to have egg smattered all over their faces. The arrogance of these elements stems from lack of understanding of the history of the region in the years leading to the partition of the sub-continent into India & Pakistan, The British in 1947 believed primacy in religion and not language should be the foundation for nationhood, the division occurred as Hindu India & a Muslim West & East Pakistan (now Bangladesh). The Sangh Parivar very well knows about the herculean efforts taken by SardarVallabhai Patel- the first home minister of Independent India in convincing the many number of princely states to renounce their rights & join the Indian union. But for the statesmanship of Sardar Patel & Jawarharlal Nehru the birth of the modern socialist Indian state would have remained a pipe dream.

The last few years have been horrific for the Indian state due to systematic attacks on institutions, demoralisation of the stature of the administration & dissent handled in the most undemocratic manner—all the adjectives which are etched proudly on the sleeves of the Sangh Parivar's forces-the term forces is relevant because they have equated themselves to the country's military in terms of preparedness for a war with an unknown enemy.

The clamour for gau-mata worship is feverishly picking up in the cow-belt of the country & the trend has proved disastrous for more than once for the minorities especially the Muslims. It is a well known fact that even among the non-vegetarian Hindus, eating beef is a taboo borne out of a religious sentiment attached to gau-mata. There is however an exception even among some Hindus-because Dalits & Keralites are not averse to consuming buffalo meat. There is no such restriction for the minorities especially the Muslims to consume the dish as a staple food. The rising religious extremism however has specifically targeted this community leading to lynching of innocents on the grounds of possessing/consuming beef. Even the traders who bought the cattle from a fair with all legitimate papers have been lynched on suspicion of smuggling the cows.

The hypocrisy of the perverts stands exposed in the case of people of North East & Goa, whose consumption of beef poses no problem to the Sangh Parivar. These incidents have been occurring with unfailing regularity & the studied silence of the ruling establishment has only increased the fear among the people into believing that the ruffians continuously run amok with blessings of their patrons who are unfortunately the law makers in their respective states. Nobody has the right in a democracy to dictate to the others, their food choices, what to eat & what not to eat. Mahatma Gandhi himself a vegetarian referring to a Muslim friend who ate beef-said that since Hinduism does not permit any Hindu from eating beef he wondered how the same yardstick could be applied to his Muslim friend when his religion permitted him to consume beef. Mahatma Gandhi was a man with thoughts which were far ahead of his times & looks like that if he had lived today-he would have been even more relevant to India than he was in those years leading to our Independence in 1947.

The politics of the cow as we should say is quite rampant particularly in the states of Uttar Pradesh, Rajasthan and Madhya Pradesh specifically in pockets where the concentration of the minorities is quite significant. The actions precipitated by the right wing elements & their moronic subjects, the gau-rakshaks is apparently more focussed on building up a smear/hate campaign against the minorities rather than being genuinely interested in the welfare of the holy cow. The gau-rakshak's conviction to hold on to their religious beliefs-will without doubt be demonstrated if each of them is vested with the responsibility of taking care of atleast one cow in their backyard. If the right wing elements proposed to execute such an idea-due to the enormous love for the cows-without doubt all the gau-rakshaks shall run for cover and vanish off from the spot. These incidents have been very disturbing to say the least & have been striking hard at the heart of India and allowing a chaotic situation to flourish-creating a deep sense of fear and despair among the minorities.

Love jihad, a popular axiom in the Sangh Parivar'sarmour is also causing needless controversies in the Hindi belt. This is a clear case of discrimination in the modern context with the ire being directed at the minorities. Love jihad can be applicable according to these goons, only if a Muslim man befriends a Hindu woman/ or the other way around & take their relationship to the next level. In most of the cases, the Muslim man becomes the culprit for having enticed the Hindu woman into his fold. The concept of consenting adults in a democracy does have no place in this relationship and the Muslim man is framed as the accused in the love Jihad, even if the Hindu woman fights to assert her genuine love for the man-the whole matter falls into deaf ears- & the issue has been adjudicated by the right wing elements outside the courts.

If the Love jihad has according to the Sangh Parivar, unfortunately culminated into a marriage-the couple is ostracized, and in the worst case the Muslim man is lynched under suspicious circumstances. If the inter faith love or marriage is the other way around-that is a Hindu man vis a vis a Muslim woman the rules do not apply as it does in the former case. The fact is it is luckily treated as inter faith marriage and has on my occasions escaped the wrath of obnoxious muddle headed goons. It is becoming obvious by the day that the Sangh Parivar is more concerned about the honour of their women & more so breeds a lot of contempt for men from the minority communities. The silence of the officialdom in all these states & also the visit of a former Central minister to the family of the accused in one of the several lynching incidents has raised several eyebrows in the media circles. These actions definitely send a wrong signal to the people of India who value peace, brotherhood & camaraderie and more so secularism as integral to co-existence in India. It goes without saying that the systematic damage is being done knowingly or unknowingly by the Sangh Parivar to the polity-which was once assumed to be the normal or solid or impervious. It doesn't seem all that sustainable now-with the continued unabashed onslaught by the RSS entities.

Whenever the intelligentsia, liberals & the intellectuals took up these issues vociferously, they were silenced into submission and have since gone into hibernation. For every topic under the sun-the Sangh Parivar has its own interpretation with a definite application of the sanskaari norms which should also put the ancient Indian mathematician Aryabhata to shame. One such issue that ruffled the feathers of the Sangh Parivar was the preaching of tolerance by the liberals & right thinking citizens & also manifested in a series of incidents involving a popular & eminent Bollywood star. The Bollywood actor has been a mainstay in the Industry for more than 30 years now-and also belonging to the minority community, married to a hindu, had in a conclave organized by a media group, expressed his displeasure at the rising intolerance in the country, probably due to various instances of lynching in the name of the cow & many other occasions where the minorities have been at the receiving end, at the hands of the saffron brigade for no fault of theirs. In this context the actor went a step further to divulge the details of a private conversation had with his wife to the reporter, which dwelt on the subject of whether the actor & his family should relocate to a place outside India.

This interview & its contents, given the stature of the actor sent shock waves across the country. The unintelligent supporters of the Sangh Parivar misunderstood the actor's pronouncement of rising intolerance in certain sections as demeaning the entire country itself & went on a war path against the actor. The majoritarian mindset was clearly on display-with many indicating that, but for the majority's benevolence the actor of his stature could have never become a superstar. It was humiliation at its worst for an actor who has won plaudits for many of his movies and couple of them have also showcased his patriotism in ample measure to the viewers. The actor said nothing wrong and was only commenting on his part about the sad state of affairs brought about by the mentality in certain sections of society. It was absolutely appalling to note, that none of the fellow actors/or the industry came to his defence & thereby denigrating the integrity & the character of film industry as well.

The TV shows in all channels & especially the ones which were patronised by the Sangh Parivar took no time to blow this issue out of proportion and in a systematic way dealt a body blow that indirectly rendered a character assassination of the actor. Some channels which were always notorious for supporting the ruling establishment, come what may, did all that was necessary to make the actor come out with a clarification that whatever he meant was construed out of context. A classic example where freedom of speech, thought, expression are no more absolute, and comes at a price.The speech that endorses the establishment doesn't require mutilation, but the one that is even slightly critical requires a refinement, the one that has made the person in question develop cold feet should be banned after all. These are the mantras that have a finite existence in today's political space.

The majoritarian mentality harboured by the Sangh Parivar has also caused endless debates on nationalism. Nationalism means having a patriotic sentiment & loyalty to one's country, the template that forms the basis of nationalism ranges from shared history, ethnicity, language & religion etc.

With the statistical backing, that our country being comprised of 80% Hindus, the right wing elements have propelled the concept of nationalism to centre stage causing shackles to the idea of diverse thought, opinion which have been part of our democratic process. The Sangh Parivar could do well to rebalance its posture, since the idea of nationalism propounded by it, is definitely on a false notion. It should be noted that before the British came to India (i.e.) in the late 17th century, the erstwhile Indian state was existing as number of princely states, under different kings and the capacity to defend themselves from the neighbouring hostile kingdoms. They existed in Kerala, Tamil Nadu, Andhra Pradesh, Bihar, Uttar Pradesh, Rajasthan, Gujarat etc, while the influence of the invading Mughal rulers who came before the British was strong in the North, West & East of India, the South was relatively free from such influences.

It goes to say that if the British had never come to India, one could not fathom how a unified Indian state could have come into existence. This assessment is primarily due to the fact that the princely states of those days had one distinct identity that differentiated each other, the linguistic ideals formed the core of their separate entity & the same could have developed into a clamour for independent linguistic states in the early 20th century. The British footprint into India first as East India company & slowly encompassing the whole of India, made the local Indians including the one that represented the princely states look upon the British as an alien & slowly movements to free themselves from British imperialism commenced from the late 19th century. The early 20th century saw the galvanization of the freedom movements, under the able leadership of Mahatma Gandhi who was able to marshall all the linguistic groups in his fight against the British and achieve the independence on August 15th 1947. We cannot speculate history, if the British had not come, how & when modern India would have evolved. It could always have been a puzzling riddle. The Sangh Parivar should realize that religion is not the major unifier & is definitely not the most important pillar for nationhood. The organization should study the example of Europe & the countries constituted in it. With the exception of Great Britain & Scandinavian countries all the European countries are land locked with a Euro rail connecting the capitals of all the countries & they exist as separate nations only.

Europe is almost 100% Christian & it is the religion of the majority like in India where majority Hindus form a chunk of the population. Now going by the saffron brigade's hypothesis where their definition of nationhood is dictated by unity in religion, is it possible to draw a parallel with Europe which should also have been a unified country like India. Conversely Europe is made up of Portugal, Spain, France, Germany, Poland, Italy & so on and, all the countries are divided on linguistic lines. It should be noted that linguistic chauvinism runs very high in the European countries as in some of the states of India. In countries like Belgium, where Dutch & French are spoken by the people, both the ethnic groups cannot see eye to eye on many issues and there is a separate Dutch & French quarter in the capital city Brussels. Of late the Catalans in Spain a Linguistic minority in that country are demanding Independence from the Spanish authority with Barcelona as their capital. The constitution of the Indian state is akin to that of Europe. People speaking different languages such as Hindi (predominantly spoken) in 8 states, Bengali, Marathi, Gujarati, Telugu, Tamil, Malayalam, Kannada, Odia etc are all existing and living under an identity called India. The existence of India as unitary structure despite all the diversity that has been pointed out, is due to many factors including the presence of the British in India, which angered & united the local population and a man of the stature of Mahatma Gandhi & the first Indian government post independence which had a thorough understanding of multi ethnic,pluralistic India & as such introduced the concept of linguistic states, to enable all the linguistic groups to preserve their language, culture & identity without having to succumb to the dominance of any particular linguistic group.

This federal structure is still in place & the extra push given by the Sangh Parivar to everyone, to arduously wear nationalism on their sleeves is an intentional malice, which will not go down well with a diverse population in India. When its is clear that religion was not the criterion for nationhood in

Europe, the Sangh Parivar should also realize that in the same manner if religion is put on the back burner in India, it could be seen that the North Indians living in Punjab, Haryana, Rajasthan, MP, UP & Bihar have a lot in common with the Pakistanis living in Punjab, Sindh, Balochistan & NWP sharing the same cuisine, customs & more importantly language, than with the South Indians. The foundation of India & Pakistan is based on a flawed concept of nationhood & it could be better if the rabid elements desisted from reinforcing the concept of nationalism on any platform.

The most worrisome fallout of the Sangh Parivar aggressively brandishing its nationalistic fervour is the fear it has created in the minds of minorities, for whom this country with its secular polity was a pride to their existence. The compulsion to chant the slogan "BHARAT MATA KI JAI" is increasing by the day, irrespective of the context,its necessity is orchestrated by the Sangh Parivar. The people who are reluctant to oblige are simply beaten up & made to fall in line by the goons. One of the motives to feed the concept of nationalism to the people by the Sangh Parivar is create as what they call "ONE INDIA – ONE THOUGHT." One wonders whether in a country of 1. 25 billion, where there is a huge deficit to create a common ground to unite people, who are unique & diverse to the core, nationalism as an issue cannot be a point of focus to unite people. If this huge country, were speaking one single language from Punjab to TN & Gujarat to West Bengal, it goes without saying that the nationalist/Patriotic sentiment will be uniform based on the loyalty to their language, but in present day Indian context nationalism will fail to create any ripples because it appeals differently to various ethnic groups.

The Sangh Parivar for years,has been highlighting the plight of the Kashmiri Pandits (Hindus) who have been displaced by the Muslim militants and have been living like refugees in their own country. The RSS & BJP have come down heavily on the opposition parties for paying scant attention to the plight of Hindu brethren from Kashmir & accusing the parties of only being concerned about the plight of the minorities in the country anytime & every time. It goes without saying that the action of the Muslim militants to evict the Kashmir pandits is unconstitutional, unacceptable & any government of the day at the centre has a moral obligation to make them safely return to their homes. These kind of incidents however do not give a free hand to Hindu religious fundamentalists to kidnap rape & kill an 8 year old girl from the minority community-which created a huge uproar in the country. The incident called the kathua rape of an innocent girl child was widely covered by the national media & for once even some of the vehemently pro-Sangh Parivar channels had to resort to some fair reporting of the incident. The ruling government at the centre was as usual insensitive to the issue, since the whole episode did not concern about the life of a person from the majority community. When questioned about this outrage, some spokespersons were even brash to the extent wondering as to why to there was no similar uproar in the country when girls from majority community in Assam were raped by infiltrators from a neighbouring country. The problem relating to Jammu & Kashmir has been a kind of status quo since 1990 when militancy erupted in the valley. At the end of the UPA-II tenure in 2014, there was a semblance of order & sanctity in the valley with things seemingly falling in place to ensure normalcy. The UPA-II Prime Minister put his best foot forward & constituted a 5 Member committee to submit a report after studying all problems on hand as far as Kashmir was concerned.

The committee went about the task in a highly professional manner, spoke even to separatists & completed an elaborate exercise by compiling & submitting the detailed report, for action regarding Jammu & Kashmir. Unfortunately the UPA-II rule had come to an end & it was up to the next government to take a call on this sensitive report which gave various recommendations to provide a healing touch to the State of Jammu & Kashmir. As was being done to every issue regarding matters of national importance, the whimsical ways of the present government put paid to any hopes of creating a fresh approach to resolve the burning issue of this state. Consequently the invaluable report is gathering dust & is yet to see the light of the day. Instead the Sangh Parivar is keen to extend the idea of "ONE INDIA & ONE THOUGHT" to the State of Jammu & Kashmir. The scrapping of special status accorded to Kashmir is one among the many plans that have been put in place as part of the Hindutva agenda for Kashmir.

The Sangh Parivar has always got the habit of history wrong. If it were in the know of things it would have definitely not have come up with the demand. At the time of partition of India, which the British had carried out on religious lines (Pakistan & present day Bangladesh) were West & East Pakistan with India sandwiched between the two provinces of the same country. Applying the same logic, a Muslim majority Kashmir should have been acceded to Pakistan, but the then ruler of Kashmir wished to make a choice between India & Pakistan, he was ready to accede to any country which gave his province special powers & status. The founding fathers of Pakistan outrightly rejected the demands. The Indian side was however willing to accept the demands & that was the history of unification of Kashmir with India. It's another story that in 1948, Pakistan invaded & occupied a part of Kashmir which is still known as POK (Pakistan Occupied Kashmir). The Sangh Parivar should have definitely known about the truth of the matter & the truth is if in 1947, the Indian government had not acceded to Kashmir's demands we would have never ever be debating about an issue called Jammu & Kashmir .

Now that there is a problem in hand, intelligence demands the resolution of the same at the earliest, but the government has complicated matters further and the situation is scarier than ever before. The Sangh Parivar wants a Muslim majority state to be a part of India & on the other hand places severe dietary restrictions on the minorities by ensuring that beef has been taken off their menu, citing reasons that it offended the religious belief of the majority community. This will definitely send the wrong signals to the Muslim majority Kashmir who shall be wondering as to how their interests shall be served under a government which is espousing a virulent Hindutva agenda. The concept of reasoning, which even an ordinary employee of private/government organization is able to apply, seems to be a distant reality for the stooges of saffron brigade who only seem to believe in a one-way traffic. A holistic approach to resolve the Kashmir issue can only be undertaken by a pack of liberals/intellectuals/ ex service men who understand Kashmir like the back of their hand.

It is advised that the Sangh Parivar does not further complicate matters in Kashmir so that it does not go to a point of no return. The obsession with religion & the attempts to trivialize Hinduism through the concept of Hindutva by the self anointed messiahs has serious consequences for the Indian Union. It is absolutely disgusting to note that the Sangh Parivar seems to believe that they are the only legitimate people to represent Hinduism. It is a matter of utter shame for the majority Hindus of this country who are well educated & understand the designs of the Sangh Parivar. Just like Hinduism, Sangh Parivar represents an upper caste hegemony, the whole religion is bundled with riddles & does not really conform to a monotheistic religion as Buddhism, Christianity or Islam. The entire faith is built upon the basis of caste which belittles the very concept of equality. The rigid caste system from time immemorial of the Hindu religion,has created a deep division in the Hindu society. Despite the constitutional guarantees provided for the upliftment of the socially backward, especially Dalits – their lot continues to be appalling even 70 years after independence. It is an irony of sorts, that despite the inherent contradictions, the right wing elements are trying to indulge in a hopeless exercise of uniting all the Hindus. All people in a religion can unite only if there is a sense of equality at least socially even if not economically. This infact is a problem for the saffron brigade which is fully aware that its attempt will be absolutely futile.

The concept of caste forms the backbone for the existence of Hinduism, if the caste structure is dismantled to forge the so called Hindu unity by the Sangh Parivar-the religion shall meet its waterloo the very next day. The Sangh Parivar which is undoubtedly the domain of the upper castes, should work to ward off the social evils which continue unabated in the Hindu society & strive to establish a classless society which can become a reality, if not now-atleast in the next 25 years. There should presumably be a realistic time frame on condition that liberal mindsets form a majority by adopting socio-economic patterns relevant to the Indian sub-continent & implement them in a relentless manner. If the whiff of change does not happen even in the longer duration of the next 25 years, then the state is headed for a sure shot turbulence & immense dissatisfaction among the marginalized in the subsequent period. The Sangh Parivar is only one of the elements along with a variety of factors that aid & abet the continuing caste discrimination all over India. Apart from the drawback of the caste structure which is a huge stumbling block in the right wing elements effort to forge Hindu unity, the linguistic divide is also an important factor which comes in the way of the Sangh Parivar's improbable aspirations.

In the southern states, especially Karnataka & Tamil Nadu, water wars over Cauvery have been almost regular. Similarly Karnataka & Andhra Pradesh have been grappling with disputes along their borders for decades now. Tamil Nadu & Kerala have a stand-off on Mullaiperiayar for several years now. Punjab & Haryana have water sharing problems which get eased now & then on a temporary basis. Karnataka & Maharashtra are battling on the status of Belgaum, a city having a substantial Marathi speaking population on the Karnataka-Maharashtra border. With regional/linguistic passion running very high in both states the state of Karnataka went to the extent of renaming the city as Belagavi in lineage with Kannada edicts. The Sangh Parivar which takes pride in fostering the attempts to sensationalize religion & thereby bring all Hindus under one agenda irrespective of language, caste, & creed should first put out its gameplan in tackling these ticklish questions regarding language/caste in the Hindu system. Similarly apart from show of linguistic chauvinism among the Hindus, there is a fervent display of caste consolidation & violence by certain communities to ensure that benefits are extended to them by the government in the form of reservations.

In Gujarat, a community which is found to be industrious, robust & enterprising went on the offensive demanding that their community also be provided with special benefits such as reservation in educational institutions & government enterprises. This community forms a whopping 16% of the total population in the state & is a dominant community in all spheres of life in the state. The state is still restive on this issue, with the matter having been put on hold by the community, in order to reap political dividend at the right time. The irony of the matter is that this community has its domination almost complete in every sense of the word, the demand for reservation may have stemmed from the fear of the fact that it's hold & influence over businesses & politics may wane due to a multitude of factors.

In Haryana as well, a community mostly agrarian & with its population spread across Uttar Pradesh, Rajasthan & Punjab as well, launched a similar kind of agitation to bring to the forefront the so called vagaries haunting them and for not being provided reservation in education & jobs etc. This community also displayed the same kind of intensity, if not more as their counter parts in Gujarat, rendering enormous amount of damage to public property. This community is naturally known for their aggressive mindset & the violence unleashed by them in this matter did not surprise many of the observers who were keenly following this matter. Apart from the major agitations mounted by the dominant communities in the two states, there have also been agitations by other communities to a much lesser degree in some states with the demand to also include them in the reserved category.

The burning issue of caste discrimination, which occurs in almost all the Indian states with increasing demeanour year on year, in the form of honour killings & continued atrocities on the Dalit population receives absolutely no response from the religiously right Sangh Parivar. It is of course true-that it is not fair to blame the Sangh Parivar alone in this matter-because the firmly entrenched caste mindsets have existed for centuries in the Hindu society & to take the bull by its horns even the 70 years of independence is not sufficient.

The attempts to integrate the diverse Hindu society were sown by the Sangh Parivar by trying to create a national sentiment, a Hindu one by upping the ante for construction of Ram Temple on the disputed site at Ayodhya. The matter propped up for the first time in 1984, when the then Congress Prime minister, opened the gates of the Babri Masjid which existed then & performed shilanyas to the Ram idols, which purportedly were bought & installed in the Masjid premises, Apart from the above the then government, also allowed the telecast of the mega serial "Ramayana" on Doordarshan, the government's national channel & the only one available for viewership throughout India. The government had only the right intention in allowing the broadcast of the epic on Lord Ram. With the glory of Lord Ram slowly penetrating the drawing rooms of Indians (North Indians) especially, a perfect platform was created for the Sangh Parivar to revive the demand for construction of the Ram temple in Ayodhya. The case in point was the demand by the saffron brigade to build the temple at the same site, where the Babri masjid existed. It was a different aspect that the Babri masjid was in a state of disuse altogether. The reason as to why the Sangh Parivar staked a claim to the site was, according to the RSS history the Masjid was an illegitimate structure & was built by the arrogant invading Mughal king Babar around 400 years ago, by demolishing the Ram Temple, that rightfully existed in that place during that period.

The minority community was aghast at this claim & the committee representing the precincts of the Babri Masjid was unwilling to trade in the site to the Sangh Parivar which claimed that such a gesture by the minority community would go a long way in fulfilling the aspirations of millions of Indians (including the ones struggling to make a living everyday, ones who had no access to housing, sanitation & the ones who could not afford 3 square meals a day). From the year 1989, the only focus of the Sangh Parivar was to build a Ram Temple in Ayodhya & all the attempts to communalize the atmosphere was carried out with full vigour.

During those times, when there were no 24x7 cable television networks, all the reportage with respect to this sensitive issue was done in the national news papers which continue to enjoy good patronage even today because of their subjective coverage of all the pressing problems facing the nation. The years 1990 & 1991 were very turbulent in India's largest state of Uttar pradesh —with BJP already having installed its government in the state by using the Ram Janmabhoomi issue to the hilt. The year 1990 especially saw the Sangh Parivar-captalize to a large extent in this matter & could be categorized as the year of rathyatras-deliberately planned to evoke the sentiments of the majority community on this issue and polarize the Indian population in the north on communal lines. The atmosphere was so much charged in the Hindi speaking states —that post 1991 general elections —when a Congress coalition came to power at the centre-a considerable amount of pressure was mounted by the right wing parties for construction of Ram temple at the disputed site. The situation become volatile with the Sangh affiliates such as VHP, Bajrang dal etc. issuing a clarion call to karsevaks from all over the country to assemble in Ayodhya-to reclaim the rightful birth place of Lord Ram & construct a temple complex.

The newspapers during those times carried out articles regarding the impending problem every other day and a chaotic situation which was bound to spiral out of control was emerging without doubt. The then Congress Prime minister – not known to be suave, but notorious for keeping silent on a multitude of important issues till the controversies died down was trying to do an encore in this matter as well. The momentum to create violence & anarchy reached a threshold, when thousands of karsevaks converged on Ayodha –despite the prohibitory orders clamped by the state government. On December 6th 1992 the zealots pulled down the Babri masjid in the most atrocious manner to the utter disbelief of the comity of world nations –who for long had a great admiration for the secular polity of the Indian state. The Central government – adopted knee jerk measures by dismissing the BJP government at the state-and was under the misconception that the issue would die a natural death. The demolition of the Babri Masjid which can be defined as India's first terrorist attack on a religious identity broadly defined the contours of the degradation of morality & lack of rational thinking among the opportunistic Indian politicians.

During those times, when Indians, the majority of whom remained largely secular-with abundant reasoning skills –the dastardly act of demolition of Babri Masjid invited large scale condemnation from all right thinking Indians as well as the Indian diaspora abroad. An eye for an eye can never be a solution to the important problems faced by the people in the country. The Sangh Parivar justified the act of pulling down the mosque-by quoting the history written in RSS textbooks. Even if all of us buy the Sangh Parivar's argument regarding the demolition, the moot question is whether, we in the 21st century belong to the barbaric times of the 16th century-to perpetrate an uncivilised act, much to the dismay of the Indians during that time. This incident can be vividly recounted by present day Indians who are 45 years & above along with the turbulence that the country faced as an aftermath of this cowardly act. The young Indians who are 25 to 39 years old & who represent the transformational India-have no knowledge of the tactics adopted by the Sangh Parivar to bring BJP to the driver's seat at the centre. They have vociferously supported the idea of change which they presumed that the right wing government would represent since 2014 & their hopes are also vanishing into their air, -and a strong belief that Sangh Parivar is nothing but a wolf in sheep's clothing is slowly beginning to reinforce in their minds.

The Barbri Masjid demolition is a gory chapter in the history of Independent India-and about a quarter century since then there seems to be no solution to the dispute. The urgency & the haste which the Sangh Parivar showed in the demolition of the structure-was not shown in their interest to construct a Ram Temple on the existing site. In the final analysis, however it looks as though that the right wing elements were keen to pull down the Babri Masjid than to build a Ram Temple there- & keep the communal pot boiling to reap rich electoral dividends. Whatever said & done, the Ram Janmabhoomi-Babri Masjid-issue continues to hold centre stage as far as the Sangh Parivar is concerned and right wing elements blatantly misused religion to exploit the sentiments of the majority, and thereby accrued its benefit at the time of the elections. The Sangh Parivar continues to vitiate the communal harmony-by indirectly propagating the concept of majoritarianism wherein, the minorities especially the Muslims have started categorizing themselves as second class citizens even without a whimper of protest.

One of the trump cards in the Sangh Parivar arsenal, apart from the perpetual display of majoritarianism is drumming up support for a co ordinated hate campaign against Pakistan, a Muslim Pakistan for that matter. Several years into their independence, both India & Pakistan continue to be at loggerheads, with lasting peace continuing to be a distant dream. On a couple of occasions when both the the nations came closer to clinching a deal, -the countries blamed the religious extremists on both sides- & said that they had to take the responsibility for stalling the peace process. While India blamed a host of extremist organisations propped up by Pakistan's powerful army & its notorious intelligence agency ISI-Pakistan squarely blamed the Sangh Parivar headed by the RSS for playing spoilsport.

The Sangh Parivar till this day- has been preaching the false sense of nationalism for quite too long & is continuously banking on a massive uproar by the majority against the so called atrocities perpetrated by Pakistan. The saffron brigade could do well to understand that both Indian & Pakistan are faced with a number of problems-which are in a way common to both the countries. Poverty is a major problem in both the countries with more than 50% of the population in both the countries leading a life which cannot be termed as comfortable in any sense. People are deprived of nutrition, housing, sanitation, health care & the human development index is abysmally low in both the countries. It is under these adverse circumstances-that both the countries have the audacity to spend a whopping amount on their respective country's armed forces. India infact spends a mind boggling 2lakh crores on defence − the cost of which goes towards maintenance of armed forces, purchase of new equipment for defence needs etc. Both the countries are building up their nuclear arsenal as well & making the sub-continent vulnerable to nuclear warfare in future.

It is definitely a matter of logic to claim that both India & Pakistan are preparing to wage a battle against an invisible enemy. There is no doubt that both the countries went to war in 1965 (Kashmir dispute) & 1971 (liberation of East Pakistan-Bangladesh) & in 1999 India had to repulse an infiltration bid by Pakistan in kargil. The people of India & Pakistan –who are watching from the side lines-should be wondering as to why the two nations continue to have frosty relations & why no attempts are being made by either side to break the ice. The Sangh Parivar on the other hand has gone a step further - & is vocal about its concept of "AKAND BHARAT"– an idea wherein the present boundaries of the Indian state are extended to include the present state of Pakistan as well. A closer examination of the Sangh Parivar's ambitions reveal how perverse it's thoughts have been vis-à-vis the developments in the modern context. There is no doubt that-both the countries India & Pakistan have a shared history that encompasses language, culture, art etc apart from religion.

If in 1947, the British did not make religion as the basis of identity of people's nationhood-there is no doubt that the sub-continent comprising India, Pakistan, Bangladesh, Nepal & Sri lanka could have existed together as a large conglomerate. However the vision has been derailed long back & all the countries have moved on to chalk out their own programmes for development of their people. It is of utmost importance for the right wing elements in our country to stop the propaganda of Pakistan-baiting, as well as demoralizing its civilian government which is a rarity of sorts and which is trying - to rein in the powerful army & stop the cross border terrorism carried out by jihadi forces. India & Pakistan trying to outwit each other in arms race-will not do any good to prevailing tensions in the region. If both the nations divert their resources, infact a substantial portion from defence expenditure-it shall go a long way with the respective governments having sufficient budgets to bring their people out of poverty.

In the mean while it is the prerogative of the Sangh Parivar not to buttress it's anti-Pakistan sentiments to ensure that the atmosphere is not vitiated even more than what actually persists between the two countries. The need of the hour is for Pakistan to realise-that continued support to armed infiltrators from across the border into Kashmir-shall never be in the best interests of initiating a dialogue with its Indian counterpart. India for its part should always exhibit the magnanimity in relationship as an elder brother & which it displayed in abundance in pre 2014 era to diffuse the tensions and facilitate talks at regular intervals to achieve the goal of long lasting peace. Pakistan should realise that it can in no way compare itself to India in size & strength just as India cannot compare itself to China. Pakistan should come to terms with reality & hasten to strike an accord with India at the earliest & come 2030 the sub-continent should see a new-geo political alignment. It goes without saying that hardline elements in India, the Sangh Parivar & in Pakistan the JUD should be relegated to the sidelines to effect an enduring peace between the two nations.

The repeated attempts by the Sangh Parivar to adopt an indigenous Hindu way of life with an undercurrent of anti-minority sentiments was in ample display in the state of

Rajasthan. The development surrounded the release of a movie named, PADMAVATI rechristened as PADMAVAT as a compromise solution to assuage the feelings of a dominant community in Rajasthan-to whose clan the medieval queen Padmavati belonged to & for whose honour the Queen waged a battle against the invading Mughals. It was a classic example where creative freedom was under severe strain- & guarantees enshrined in the constitution, that freedom of speech, expression, thought are absolute, infact did have their, boundaries, limits in this matter as per Sangh Parivar, school of thought. The film was originally to be titled as "PADMAVATI" & directed by one of India's eminent film makers, who has to his credit many number of movies that dwelt on the subjects of the glory of India. The whole controversy started as a skirmish by the right wing elements who somehow had a premise that the director had offended their queen Padmavati's dignity by linking her to Mughal emperor Alauddin Khilji. This sparked a chain reaction in terms of violence throughout the state by the community, which demanded a complete ban on the film. The Sangh Parivar also jumped on to the band wagon to defend the community's honour, which according to it was intrinsic to the honour of the majority Hindu community as well.

The movie could not release on the scheduled date - as the wave of hooliganism unleashed by various organisations owing allegiance to the community let loose an orgy of terror on the streets in the major cities of Rajasthan, The cinema halls that had planned to screen the movie, were vandalized & the law enforcing agencies were nowhere in the picture to ensure a sense of order. The community which was originally for a total ban on the movie, finally relented and had only one demand, to rename the movie. The director after detailed deliberations with the CBFC chair person decided to name it as PADMAVAT. The director had all along been ascertaining that the movie was in no way affront to the glory of RaniPadmavati and invited the leaders of the fringe groups affiliated to the community for a special screening of the movie, so as to enable them form their subjective opinion.The desperation of the director in this matter was fully visible on a number of occasions. All the sane voices dipped to irretrievable levels with regard to enforcement of what represents the modules of right thinking in democratic India. The Sangh Parivar, including the BJP government at the centre and state were mute spectators, to the unfolding of this conundrum & infact extended tacit support to the violence fearing that an iron hand in this sensitive issue was bound to antagonise the community, which was seen as major votebank by all the parties in Rajasthan. Nobody even with the lowest levels of intelligence is able to fathom the anger of the community in question. One wondered as to whether the community was distraught at distortion of history in the name of creative freedom or was the linking of their queen with a Muslim invader was the bone of contention & unacceptable to them. The Sangh Parivar which played a meaty role in the whole episode seemed to tilt the dynamics to imply that the honour of a Hindu queen was at the mercy of a Muslim king & thereby was adding the communal tinge to the whole matter. If every community because of its caste affiliation, shall take offence to the way their community or peers are projected in visual media, it might surely be curtains down on the wonderful concept of creative freedom, which harbours liberal & progressive mindsets in every sphere of life.

The myopic vision that the Sangh Parivar reflects in matters of public interest offers a lot more scope for discussion.The world over, LGBT (Lesbian, Gay, Bisexual & Transgender) community is fighting for its rights & successfully getting its rightful existence ratified. In India, this community too, numbering at least 3.5 million has been fighting with its back against the wall, to overcome a social taboo that normally exists in a conservative country like ours. In comparison to the western nations, India had still been following the archaic law laid down by the British dating back to 1861, that criminalizes sexual activities "against the order of nature" arguably the homosexual acts. The Sangh Parivar, with its natural inclination to the extreme right was vociferous in its contention, that section 377 should be in place & granting LGBT community their right was not in conformity with the Hindu culture & dharma. The Sangh Parivar proponents also went a step further, to classify this community as people who suffered from mental illness, & required medical help to restore them to normal health condition. The state of normal implied by Sangh Parivar meant that the human beings abided by the laws of nature in their sexual orientation as well. In the year 2013 the Supreme Court upheld the constitutional validity of section 377 leaving the LGBT community high & dry, With the LGBT community's continued & resolute fight to be out of shadows under a huge cloud, the Sangh Parivar was obviously elated by the decision & commended the Supreme Court for its bold decision to keep the Indian, rather the all pervading Hindu ethos intact.

The fringe element's opposition to matters regarding LGBT rights,dates back to more than 20 years, when a Hindi movie directed by a famous woman director came under consistent attack by these groups. The film dealt with the relationship between two married women, ultimately culminating into a sexual encounter akin to lesbians. One could vividly remember the humiliation that the entire female cast of the movie including the director had to undergo at the hands of the saffron brigade. The LGBT community has however survived all the odds, especially the tirade and the continuous onslaught on it by the organizations affiliated to the Sangh Parivar. The year 2018, marked a golden chapter in the history of the LGBT community in India, when after a relentless legal battle, a review petition filed by them as a counter to 2013 SC judgment was adjudicated in their favour by the SC bench. The Supreme Court stuck down the constitutional validity of section 377 that criminalizes same sex relationship & ruled that LGBT community was entitled to the same rights as the other citizens of India & almost all the demands of LGBT community relating to their rightful existence in the public domain were also met. The Sangh Parivar has not expressed its views on the judgment as yet, since it shall be still licking its wounds vis-à-vis, the aggressive stand taken by it in this matter. When it comes to Sangh Parivar's stand of acting as the vanguard of Hinduism, it should be noted that the right wing elements have at best exhibited selective amnesia on a wide variety of issues & thereby opening, up a debate on their own contradictions.

The saffron brigade which proudly projects YOGA an Indian innovation & specifically a Hindu one, is seemingly silent on the other famous ancient Hindu innovation, KAMASUTRA. YOGA as an exercise with its therapeutic values has been embraced by almost the entire world, making the Sangh Parivar extremely proud of its Sages/gurus who had succesfully handed over this act to their successors, making the entire science of YOGA, a jewel in the crown of India. However, when it comes to discussion on Kamasutra, the Sangh Parivar maintains its stoic silence, seemingly to imply that some rogue elements in the ancient Hindu society were responsible for the development of this science. Kamasutra, in short, deals with the art of human sexuality explained in various chapters by the ancient Indian Philosopher Vatsyayana who lived in the 3rd century BC. The chapters of Kamasutra have found their way to the edifices of ancient Hindu temples in the form of exquisite stone sculptures namely on Sun temple in Orissa & khajuraho temples in Madhya Pradesh. These temples were built by the respective Hindu kings from 9th century, upto 14 century AD. The temples were abundantly embellished with sculptures, rather erotic images in various postures which were contiguous with the chapters of Kamasutra.

Along with the several images that conformed to conventional acts of sexuality, there were also few images, where a woman is seen hugging another woman in a rather compromising situation & two men facing each other in an undressed position. These exclusive images in a swarm of eroticism cannot definitely be seen as acts of perversion by the sculptor, or by the Hindu rulers of the times who patronised the art. The presence of these images symbolised unnatural sexuality, in Sangh Parivar's school of thought. It only reinforces the claims made by historians that homosexuality as a sexual practice existed in India, although at a miniscule level. We are really fortunate that all our Hindu rulers of the past have been liberal at best, with admirable respect for art & architecture, as seen in the design & construction of temples dedicated to various gods all over the country. If the ruler had believed that the concept of homosexuality was not acceptable, it would have definitely not found a way for depiction in some of the famed temples of India. The Sangh Parivar either knowingly or unknowingly has been trapped in a paradoxical situation.

On the one hand it gives an impression that it knows everything about Hinduism like the back of its hand, while seemingly it is woefully ignorant & illiterate about the ancient history of Hinduism, which to this day hasn't evolved much & has faithfully handed over its traditions to the ensuing generations. The Sangh Parivar's approach to all issues related to its religion smacks of hypocrisy at the highest level. The pracharaks are using the ideals of religion to their convenience, like a dagger taken out of an unconventional armoury, to frighten the minorities & consolidate their brand called "MAJORITARIANISM". It will always continue to be a million dollar question as to whether hardcore supporters of the Sangh Parivar will consent to an open, intellectual debate on Hindu religion, since most of their ideas about this near liberal faith seem to be concocted & half-baked in the real sense. The Sangh Parivar may still file a review petition against the 2018 SC judgment on LGBT rights to have its way on this issue and stimulate a perverted thought process in the country which unfortunately is working to its advantage. In such an eventuality, it shall without doubt prove its poor understanding of the subject in the Indian Hindu context vis-a-vis the situation that prevailed with respect to subject of sexuality in ancient India.

The Indian woman has always been centrist to the ideology of Sangh Parivar, infact the programme of "BETI BACHAO – BETIPADAO" a brain child of the present government, is a good initiative to help in the emancipation of women living in the rural areas & ensure gender equality, and independence to achieve their major life goals. The Sangh Parivar however visualises the growth of Indian women in the sanskaari traditions of India. Every other day crimes are reported, mostly rapes from many places in North India & safety of women has also become a major problem. The Sangh Parivar has never openly condemned these incidents of serial rape & assault on women – in the manner it was holding the cudgels for matters involving the woes of the majority Hindus. This only goes to highlight the fact that gender discrimination takes place with such effortless ease in our society, the checks & balances that have been put in place to contain the violence have failed to deter the offenders. The Sangh Parivar has always soft pedalled on issues relating to Indian women ranging from their emancipation, independence, moreover the right to express their feminist ideals as their counterparts in the West.

The saffron brigade is allergic to women who are intelligent, who speak their mind on a host of issues and that are bound to bring embarrassment to the Indian men. In short the prismatic view of the Indian women from the Sangh Parivar's perspective, is that of one who is faithful to her husband & his family, religious, virtuous as Goddess Lakshmi. This mindset is typical of a religious right akin to some of the Islamic countries especially Iran- where a fundamentalist regime has curtailed the independence of women who are yearning for a liberal regime to realise their real freedom. Indian women have been unshackling male chauvinism systematically over the last 20 years, making remarkable progress in all spheres of activity, but a lot more needs to be done before they realise that they have become truly independent. The lawmakers in the previous government also proposed a 33 pc reservation for women in LokSabha/Raj Sabha. The present government has still not deemed it fit to facilitate the passage of the bill which shall go a long way in ensuring that a lot many women shall also form a major part of governance process in this country. The major obstacle is the patriarchal mindset of the Sangh Parivar which continues to trivialise and belittle the importance of women in the larger exercise of nation building. The Sangh Parivar is also vehemently opposed to the influence of western culture on young Indian women, has demonstrated its displeasure through its fringe outfits by indulging in violence to disrupt anything which in its view is alien to the Hindu tradition and culture.

Women in India are still coming out of their cocoons to fight discrimination, putting admirable efforts to rub shoulder to shoulder with men on the podium of success. The Sangh Parivar still operates on a misguided notion that all is well with the condition of its Hindu women and the present status quo in the society guarantees the women all their rights. When all is not well with the condition of Hindu women, with prejudice becoming a pervading aspect throughout India, irrespective of linguistic threshold, the right wing government has ventured into the uncharted territory of securing the rights of Muslim women & extricate them from the horrors of triple talaq, a method adopted by Muslim men to extract instant divorce from their wives. There is no denying that rights of all women, whether Hindu, Muslim, Sikh, Christian, Jain etc have to be restored to provide them honour & dignity in society, but the Sangh Parivar showing a special consideration in this matter definitely raises eyebrows.

The Muslim women definitely feel let down by certain provisions in their religion, which are discriminatory towards them and are fighting for a recourse. As for as the issue of

Triple Talaq is concerned, a remedy as such has been provided by Sangh Parivar by hastily passing an ordinance on Triple Talaq for the Muslim community. The Sangh Parivar is back to what it does best, polarisation in this case has been attempted to create a rift between the Muslim men & women on this issue, believing so it is preying for Muslim women votes, who have been a benefactor by what the Sangh Parivar terms as a historic decision. The Muslim women are surely not novices to deliberately fall into the trap set by the Sangh Parivar, although there are certain issues that are discriminatory against them in their religion, they will continue to back their men enmasse to battle the bogey of hatred let loose on them by the Sangh Parivar, which has systematically made them grudgingly accept the position of second class citizens in the Indian demography.

The Indian women should do well to realise that living under the shadow of right wing politics shall have adverse effects on their freedom as well. In many of the right wing governments, around the world, the terms like women's rights, feminism have borne the brunt of ultra-nationalists like Sangh Parivar. At this juncture one is reminded of TV debates on issues involving the women, on many occasions the members of Sangh Parivar who participated in the debates have demeaned the women representing the liberal mindsets. It goes without saying that the Sangh Parivar is definitely not comfortable with the idea of an independent free thinking, liberal minded woman in the Indian context & their portrayal of Indian women continues to be the one who is located in history & tradition & similar to the Devis – LAKSHMI & SARASWATHI.

The Indian women may be demure, but have proved their versatility on multiple occasions that they are strong willed, mentally tough than their male counterparts. In the same vein, it also goes without saying that if they had been assigned with the powers of governing the country, India would have been a better place to live & would have made much more progress than what has been achieved till date. It is therefore definitely incumbent on the Indian women to keep the Sangh Parivar's ideals at bay since it does distort the basis of equitable rights & also relegates Indian woman as second class citizens. The women have a large role to play in the coming decade to help India come out poverty, perverted, religious and discriminating mindsets towards them and to ensure prosperity and near equal distribution of wealth. The Sangh Parivar has never had a sway over the Indian women, since they have been more sensible enough to see through their gameplan than their male counterparts.

The Sangh Parivar- after ensuring that its political affiliate came to power at the centre in 2014- has launched carefully orchestrated attempts to expand its prophecy through some select television channels, which have infact become propaganda channels for the Sangh Parivar. It is true that some of the channel founders do have an affiliation to the Sangh Parivar – but their unwavering loyalty will put even the hard core bhakts to shame. These media houses & channels have taken upon themselves, to seriously drive home the point to the audience that RSS is a nationalist organisation and cannot be equated with any Muslim terror groups given the enormous amount of social service rendered by the organization. The one point agenda of these channels is to discredit the opposition which is already in a disarray and the media continues to be critical of dynastic politics of the principal opposition GOP-the Congress. These are no limits to heights of sycophancy of these channels. On a day, when many media channels were covering incidents of atrocities on Dalits in a city in Uttar Pradesh , which became a big talking point all over the country, the channels mouth piecing for the Sangh Parivar were debating the issue of cross border terrorism in Kashmir, and hosted debates on how to tame the enemy from aross the border.

The news anchors of these channels seem to have taken the viewers for granted, keep churning out illogical stuff and have made a laughing stock of themselves. These news channels of course, still have an unfinished agenda; usher in the golden rule of the Sangh Parivar forever. One of the leaders of the Sangh Parivar has proudly proclaimed that there is no opposition to them for the next 50 years in India & they shall continue to rule the roost & bring in a NEW INDIA. The already overzealous TV channels have taken note of their master's observation & are already working out a strategy to ensure their dream run. In a country of 1.25 billion, where diverse thought & opinion are the order of the day, one wonders how long these media channels shall dangerously tread on patriotism and nationalism. These media channels are

multi — taskers, if the government receives a setback in by-
elections in some states, the channels are immediately on their
toes to carry out an opinion poll and state that despite the loss
in polls, the sheen & glamour of the Sangh Parivar remained
intact. In some cases when the Sangh Parivar was hopelessly
cornered with respect to some pressing people's issues, which
was diminishing the ruling party's stature, the channels had the
habit of bringing the same people who were critical of the
government to the debate make a buffoon of them & prove
that they are puppets of the opposition parties.

The propaganda channels are a new phenomenon to the
concept of Indian politics. It is also true that some of the
media houses have been patronized by the opposition parties,
but none of them have gone overboard, deliberately attacked
the viewer's sensibilities as the Sangh Parivar channels, which
are even adept at proving truth as untruth. The concept of paid
news channels do not augur well for our democracy and is
definitely affront to the concept of free thought, rational,
analytical thinking. These channels are only bothered about
short term gains & do not realise the enormous damage they
cause to the fabric of India bypassing the journalistic ethics
that define their profession. The Sangh Parivar has apparently
caused destruction to the proud tradition of Indian journalism
— which at one point upheld the values of what the Indian
state stood for & by its impartial, subjective reporting, also
questioned the wrong doings of the government of the day,
thereby prompting them to take corrective action. It remains
to be seen as to how long these channels can continue to

operate in the so, called comfort zone with abundant patronage, support from the Sangh Parivar. However these channels anchored by some once famous journalists will seek redemption for their selfish misdeeds, because no amount of remorse shall come to their rescue. Not all the channels / media houses in the country are lap dogs of the Sangh Parivar, there are still some media houses that espouse the concept of neutrality in their news publications.

These news channels have also become wary in the last few years, over fears of facing retribution from the Sangh Parivar, if they carried any news items that was even slightly critical of its governance. It is an open secret, that if the media house maintained its independence in its reporting & even being critical sometimes about the government, it had to face, the music from the ruling establishment in the form of IT raids & cases filed by the CBI for non-compliance to the government regulations. By adopting this practice, the Sangh Parivar has ensured that it has fairly a large & friendly media – going into election mode continuously. It is definitely a pitiable sight looking, at the condition of the media houses in India, many of whom, for the sake of survival are at the mercy of unreasonable demands made by the Sangh Parivar. It is really not known as to when,a modicum of integrity reverts back to the citadel of Indian journalism as large part of it has already been mortgaged to likes of the Sangh Parivar to carry out its unfinished agenda of putting its map all over the Indian sub-continent.

Over the last 70 years India has evolved as a multi-ethnic democracy with a fairly well, entrenched federalism in place. The Sangh Parivar with its parochialism and its actions is posing a serious threat to the federalism of the country. In a large country with a rising population, the requirements, demands can be only met by the decentralisation of power, making accountability a habit till the last individual who works in the government. The State governments are dependent on the aid dished out by the Central governments, on programmes based on the State's population, the performance index with respect to delivery & disbursement. The federal structure of the country meant that the elected state government truly represented the aspirations of the respective people and is competent to take it's own decisions with conviction for the welfare of their own people. The Central government's role is only to ratify and accord the competent sanction. However over the last few years, the Sangh Parivar which continues to battle between the devil and the deep sea, as far as the understanding of the various issues, is concerned has unnecessarily interfered with the decisions of some of the State governments, thereby severely infringing on the autonomy of the State government. The State governments may have been incompetent, but that does not in any manner offer a leeway for the Sangh Parivar to redefine the Centre-State relations. In some of the states, the governors supplanted by the Sangh Parivar - & whose job is only constitutional in nature, are actively participating in governance, thereby bringing a huge embarrassment to the respective State government.

The needless interference in the governance of the states is bound to even further lower the already sinking credibility of the Sangh Parivar and shall pose a grave threat to the centre-state relations, and the concept of federalism provisioned in the constitution. In places like Delhi & Puducherry the blatant interference is there to see for the general public, leading to a considerable amount of misunderstanding between Lt Governors and the Chief Ministers. If the proposal of the governors, is to ensure a seamless governance by the government, the same shall be guaranteed by behind the door discussions, rather than generate an ugly spat in front of the public, which definitely lowers the prestige of the respective offices in the eyes of the people for whom the welfare measures are to be requisitioned and implemented. The Sangh Parivar's attempts to meddle in the respective state governments actions through its nominated governors who are invariably from its ranks, is only bound to boomerang on them creating a series of uncomfortable scenarios in the future.

A recent example of the Sangh Parivar exerting its muscle over a state government was seen in the centre versus Kerala relationship. Kerala was devastated by unprecedented floods, causing huge loss to property and infrastructure. There is no denying that help in the form of monetary aid flowed into Kerala to offset the huge catastrophe that had engulfed the state. This however was only a pittance in terms of the damage caused in thousands of crores to the state. Therefore it was natural for any Chief Minister to look forward to the central government to allocate these funds to ensure speedy rehabilitation, in extraordinary cases help from foreign donors is also welcome to mitigate the suffering of the people. In this context, the government of UAE which has a huge expatriate Keralite population and who have in a way been responsible for the vast strides of the development in the Gulf kingdom came forward to extend an aid package to the state. The centre immediately spurned the offer, citing a previous government rule of not accepting donations from foreign countries to manage natural disasters. Apart from turning down the offer the central government reiterated that our country was self reliant in funds, which shall be helpful for the state of Kerala to come out of uncertain times. The Sangh Parivar has till date played only dirty politics on this issue with the quantum aid equivalent to the one offered by the foreign government is yet to see the light of the day.

The Sangh Parivar is setting a dangerous and unforeseen precedent in centre-state relations & makes no bones of its ambitions to rewrite the federal structure of the country. The Sangh Parivar's desire to remote control the whole India operations, from a power centre in Delhi is very atrocious and sooner the realization dawns on them about the impracticality – the better it shall be for the Sangh Parivar. The concept of India is definitely its unity in diversity & it's not the other way around. The concept is so intricately woven and any attempt to even slightly tear it by the callous, nonsensical attitude of the right wing elements, in their attempts to rewrite Indian history will only seriously harm the much preserved unity and integrity of this nation of 70 years. The Sangh Parivar could find reason not to venture into choppy waters, which shall adversely affect its already damaged reputation.

The Sangh Parivar's watchful eyes, donning the cap of custodians of Hindu culture & heritage have infringed on the functioning of many institutions that have been accorded autonomous status by the erstwhile governments. One such organisation is the CBFC (Central Board of Film Certification) – the body as such wields extraordinary powers, regulates the content of Indian movies & certifies them as suitable for Adult or Universal viewership. Ever since the Sangh Parivar was in a position to influence matters and get into the thick of action in the certifying body, things have become bad to worse to the concept of artistic freedom which forms the basis for any film making. The word autonomous was only on paper and the Sangh Parivar has been successful till date to nominate its person as the Chairman of the body. The chairpersons, apart from certifying the movies, made sure that no, anti Sangh Parivar rhetoric came on board under the guise of artistic expression & clearly nipped them in the bud. In this fast moving world where the technological advances have been tremendous, it is possible to download and access content in a jiffy, the CBFC still continues to live in an old man's world. CBFC functions only in a manner to suit the whims and fancies of a certain vested political interest, has different set of rules for different people. One of the previous chairpersons of the board who was also nominated by the Sangh Parivar, effected an audacious 48 cuts to a Hindi film before categorizing it as "A" movie. The film industry was stunned by his actions & was demanding greater transparency in the operations of the CBFC. The film industry took a while to understand that the chairperson was more interested in pleasing his bosses and to uphold the sanskaari traditions, rather than give a decent account of his actions to the people.

The irony is that the chairperson was himself a Hindi film director in the 1990s and whose movies were characterized by vulgarity and sleaze in the song picturisation, objectifying, the heroines as sex symbols, sometimes even putting some X rated Hollywood movies to shame. Many Indian movies have met the same fate at the CBFC, - not receiving the needed support, at home, the eminent film directors have screened their movies at International film festivals on a regular basis and have won critical acclaim for their art of film making. Although there have been many controversies surrounding the ability to function with due diligence of the CBFC, a very recent incident comes to mind which is a reflection of primitive mindset of those in charge of shaping the destiny of our country. A Malayalam film director had to run from pillar to post for getting a certification for his movie. The CBFC had absolutely no problem with the content of his movie and agreed that is it was fit for public consumption. The CBFC had only one problem- the title of the movie which the director had named as SEXY DURGA. The director was at pains to understand as why the movie's name should be a problem at all and had never thought that he would run into a controversy with the proposed title of the movie. The CBFC on their own should have been able to take a decision in this matter but was of the view that it was surely going offend the Sangh Parivar since the name "DURGA" referred to a Hindu goddess. As it turned out to be – instructions from higher authorities implied that the movie's name SEXY DURGA was inappropriate and would hurt the sentiments of a particular community, was not acceptable in the present form. The director who literally waged a lone battle – with no support from any quarters – finally agreed to name the movie as S. DURGA – to remove all obstacles and facilitate its release. There is definitely no end to Sangh Parivar's hypocrisy, the organisation should have to realise that the names of most Indian Hindu women be it Anusha, Aparna,Subadra,Priya,Devina,Padma,Geetha etc are the names attributed to various hindu goddesses. Similarly would it have been alright for the Sangh Parivar if any of the above names were suffixed to the term SEXY in lieu of DURGA & the film got a CBFC certification. It should be mentioned that with every passing year – censorship as a tool to repress public opinion is assuming monstrous proportions, one such organisation is CBFC – which given its sweeping powers has failed to exercise its functions in a non-partisan manner. It may be recalled that the CBFC as a professional body in the 1990's & 2000's acted without fear or favour with the adjudication of a movie purely done on its merit – since most of the board members had impeccable integrity, widely travelled and also have felt the pulse of movie goers, the world over and were in a position to formulate a dictum for the passionate Indian movie goer, who was yearning for a change from commercial cinema to a more realistic movie format which discussed the problems of its people and the country. It goes without saying that board members in the 1990's & 2000's were liberal in their approach towards the acceptance of new ideas in film making and definitely were packed with more intellect to express independent opinion on a wide range of subjects – without the fear of having to get the blessings of people who were the powers to grant the authority to the members, which unfortunately is not the situation in the present context. The Sangh Parivar without doubt has an anathema – to all things modern – which its believes shall result in the erosion of the long cherished and appreciated Hindu traditions. This falsehood is surely to be overturned soon by Young India which is becoming restless by the day. As far as the film certification goes – the CBFC has only one job to do, watch the movie and certify it as viewing for "Adults Only" or Universal viewership, it has no mandate to effect cuts – since a group of individuals cannot decide what is suitable or unsuitable for the viewers, as it is a matter of perception. The entertainment should encompass movies without cuts, but generalized for viewing only by the pertinent age groups.

The Sangh Parivar has now set it sights on the issue of illegal migrants who are settled in India especially those from Bangladesh & the Rohinyga Muslims from Myanmar. One of its state governments in Assam has infact finalized an NRC (National Register of Citizens) in which it has identified a whopping 40 lakhs as illegal migrants who have settled in the state of Assam & hence forth they have been excluded from the NRC. The state of Assam has always been sensitive to the issue of migrants from other states & there have been organisations in the past that have carried out attacks on the migrants, who according to them are alien to the state. Most of the illegal migrants in Assam are Indian Bengalis,Bangladeshi Bengali speaking Muslims, Bengali speaking Rohingya Muslims from Myanmar. The Sangh Parivar has been proudly trumpeting its achievement of formation of NRC & has vowed to deport the 4 million illegal migrants to their respective countries. If the illegal migrants had been anybody except Muslim, say Nepali speaking Hindu migrants one wonders whether the exercise of preparation of NRC would have been undertaken at all. It clearly boils down to the Sangh Parivar's hypothesis, that the migrants are Muslim and they have to get out of India.

The problem of illegal migrants coming in vast numbers into the North – East of India has not happened overnight. In fact the incidents were at least several decades old & the reality is some of the migrants have settled in India for a good 50-60 years and are enjoying the benefits of Indian citizenship. In the year 1971, India went to war against Pakistan not for any cross border violation in Kashmir, but to liberate Bangladesh (then East Pakistan) from the clutches of the Army of West Pakistan. The Punjabi dominated West Pakistan army was adopting repressive measures against the Bengali speaking East Pakistan, and consequently thousands of refugees were flooding the Indian borders on the East and the Central government headed by a Congress Prime Minister had a huge problem on their hands, to stave off an imminent humanitarian disaster & to stop the flood of refugees breaching the Indian borders. The statesman like act of the Indian Army,helped in liberating Bangladesh from Pakistan and also addressed the head ache of countless number of Bangladeshi refugees infiltrating into India.

The Sangh Parivar should realise that as the world's largest democracy and one among the few countries that has a concern for human rights, India has always been seen as a place of hope for refugees from all over the world, and as such it would be imperative for India to be accommodative to the problems of human rights faced by the illegal immigrants in their respective countries such as Myanmar etc. The Sangh Parivar no doubt is desperately trying to make a poll issue out of NRC & the efforts to polarise yet again are left to the imagination of Indians. The organisation is aggressively expanding its base in W. Bengal – which has a substantial Bangladeshi migrant population, is pitching for an NRC in W. Bengal which it believes shall put the present government in a quandary. It remains to be seen whether an NRC will ever be constituted in W. Bengal and present government is willing to act against fellow Bengali speaking people from Bangladesh.

The Sangh Parivar should do well to realise – just as the Tamils in TamilNadu expressed solidarity with Sri Lankan Tamil speaking Muslims whose businesses were recently attacked in Colombo – Sri Lanka – the present government in W. bengal is likely to stand staunchly behind the Bengalis from Bangladesh, clearly demonstrating that linguistic passion and chauvinism will outsmart the Sangh Parivar's concept of nation hood based on unity of Hindus, cutting across language / caste creed. These acts of people from W. Bengal & Tamil Nadu clearly will demonstrate to the them – that language comes first and definitely the right wing does not know how to prioritise the status of religion in the hierarchy of classification to decide matters of paramount importance. The Sangh Parivar hasn't realized that the disenchanted voters in May 2014- sought a new dawn in voting for their government. The UPA-II was portrayed as a Satan of corruption by the media which unravelled its bogey of unending corruption. The people's desire was to have a clean government that protected its citizens & kept its promises with respect to the electorate. The Sangh Parivar was not voted to uphold the rights of particular community especially the Hindus.

The Sangh Parivar has been clearly plagued by lack of performance by its government—with the result an exasperation and disbelief seems to be creeping into the system. With little to showcase in terms of remarkable achievements, the Sangh Parivar has started to sow the seeds to slowly polarize the voters ahead of continuous elections—to somehow desperately hold on to the mandate once again to execute their unfinished agenda. The Indian voter, who by this time is famished, drained & at a loss of words to judge the present government seems to be waiting patiently as all his agony has fallen into deaf ears. The Sangh Parivar should work on alternative strategies to hoodwink the Indian voter—since it can be safely vouched that the Indian voter shall not fall a prey to dirty game of polarized politics time and again.

The Sangh Parivar has been wrong footed yet again by the Supreme Court judgment on entry of women pilgrims of all ages into Sabarimala Temple in Kerala. As per convention the Sabarimala temple is open to all men and girls (upto 10 years) and women (above 50 years) implying that women in the age group of 10—50 are not allowed to worship Lord Ayappa who is a celibate. A case filed in the Supreme court, pressed for entry of women of all ages into the Sabarimala Temple , called for gender equality and the right to pray for all Hindu women. After marathon deliberations in this matter the Supreme court has ruled that women of all ages can indeed enter Sabarimala to worship Lord Ayappa & also instructed the temple authorities to make adequate arrangements to accommodate the large number of women pilgrims who were expected to visit the temple complex because of this verdict. The double speak of the Sangh Parivar on this issue was too obvious to miss—initally after welcoming the SC verdict it retracted after the sentiments of the Hindu community in Kerala were against the entry of women of all ages into Sabarimala temple.

The Sangh Parivar is now spear heading some of the protests against the SC ruling in Kerala & has requested the ruling Left front government (for whom religion is never a part of its appetite) to file a review petition against the SC decision to allow all women into Sabarimala. The left government immediately took a swipe at the Sangh Parivar & said that in 2006 it was the Sangh Parivar that filed a petition in the Supreme court to allow women of all ages into the Sabarimala, putting the outfit in a state of discomfiture. This is one clear example as to how the organisation continues to change its stance on a wide variety of subjects relating to national importance like a chameleon. The SC ruling in this matter has elicited two views from the same Sangh Parivar initially & now the organization is involved in fire fighting to douse and minimize the damage. In the meantime agitations are being held by various Hindu groups, protesting against the Supreme Court decision to allow women of all ages into Sabarimala temple complex post the verdict - whether, women in the age group of 10-50 years will dare to venture into the complex to offer their prayers remains to be seen. The Sangh Parivar which has been repeatedly snubbed electorally in the state, is trying to latch on to the religious Hindu sentiment and in the process trying to lay the foundation for the saffron brigade to set its foot in Kerala.

The past experience & patterns have shown that highly educated Kerala values freedom, liberty, cultural identity very close to it's heart, and since these terms have nothing in common with saffron brigades analogy, it is any body's guess as to how it's electoral fortunes could take shape in the state of Kerala. The Supreme court ruling in the Sabarimala case opened a Pandora box, it should be noted that the petition was not filed by a woman devotee from Kerala or for that matter any of the southern states. The petitioner would have had no idea of history of Sabarimala temple & the traditions that have been followed till date, to maintain the so called sanctity of the temple. Sabarimala temple is not an isolated case alone,it has shot into the limelight because it is one of the popular Hindu pilgrimage centres like Varanasi and Lord Venkateswara temple in Tirupati. There are many temples in the states all over India & almost all of them do have some rules which the devotees are only too happy to follow. The contention of all the authorities is that these are age old rules and should not be broken. The Sabarimala Temple issue can also be treated in the same manner for the sake of upholding history, tradition and sanctity of the temple complex. The solution to the crux of problems faced by the temple boards irrespective of the states, is the interference of the government in managing it's day today affairs. The government should free the temple boards of political control, influences and allow them to function in an independent manner.

The Sangh Parivar should be primarily held responsible for bringing religion into the public domain. In a secular country, politicians and the political parties should refrain & keep themselves away from matters of religious importance. The Supreme court would have only reluctantly passed its orders in the Sabarimala case, since religious matters have become free for all due to excessive interference by the Sangh Parivar. But for the forcible insertion of religion into the public plat form, all the matters of religious importance could have been decided by the respective religious bodies, whether Hindu, Muslim, Christian or Sikh and the only option left for the political parties and the court of the land was to respect them. The Sangh Parivar has undoubtedly set an unhealthly trend, which is definitely a monster in the making, the right wing affiliates lack foresight and the intellect to diffuse this controversy, which only a states man like approach can ensure a logical closure. The bad example set by Sangh Parivar in pandering to religious sentiments & thereby trying to make religion a part of staple diet of every Indian should be forthwith rejected.

The 2014 general elections was a water shed, with the Sangh Parivar's BJP-while winning a clear majority on their own, were not dependent on the pre-poll allies for the formation of the government at the centre. In the run-up to the elections the Sangh Parivar put up an election-blitzkrieg where it highlighted the innumerable number of scams during the UPA-II period, successfully and was able to hold a considerable sway over the people. The Sangh Parivar should be reminded that none of their cards which were colorfully painted with communal agenda such as the Construction of Ram Temple, abolition of triple talaq, uniform civil code took the centre stage at the time of the campaign. In fact Sangh Parivar was careful enough to see that these issues were put on the back burner, to enable them transform into a pan Indian entity.

The Sangh Parivar clearly fought the elections on two planks, development & rooting out corruption.The people disenchanted with widespread allegations of corruption against the UPA-II government saw a ray of hope in the tall promises made by BJP and voted them to power. After completion of one term, the government is not able to showcase a single achievement in an elaborate manner to the general public. Instead, an exercise of mud-slinging between the ruling and opposition parties, dots the headlines of all the major newspapers in the country. The present government which was shouting from over the rooftops, exposing the corruption, misdeeds of the previous UPA-II government, also seems to be taking decisions symptomatic of crony capitalism, and thereby adding credence to accusation of corruption by the opposition parties.

The Indian Corporates, are seen to be very comfortable with the neo-liberal policy of the Sangh Parivar's government conforming to free market economy & have no other consideration except to fill in their deep pockets. The Corporates have definitely wanted a change of government at the centre- & in 2014 have effected it by pouring thousands of crores into the Sangh Parivar's coffers to help them in the election campaigns. Due to massive contribution of funds, within a short period by people who identified themselves with the Sangh Parivar ideology, BJP was able to build its party headquarters, one of the largest in Asia within no time. The party also had to ensure a payback time to the long list of Corporates who had handsomely contributed to it's election fund, the result being swinging the offset contract of a military deal in favour of a known business house, which is already battling bad debt. The ploy of the government in the deal seems to be of one that bailed out one of the illustrious names in the industry & also made available funds to its party ahead of the season of elections. Another example was the award of Rs. 1000 crores to a bigger Industrial house for an yet to be established University of Eminence. The dark reality of the

Sangh Parivar is that it is protecting the same tenets, against which it vociferously lent its voice during the UPA-II regime.

The Sangh Parivar's proud claims that there have been no instances of corruption & that nothing has been reported in the mainstream media,is definitely an insult to the intelligence of the average Indian. The Sangh Parivar that was very critical of the previous UPA-II government's various misadventures as far as corruption was concerned, should walk the talk & ensure transparency in all the deals made by the government in big ticket purchases. If any serious allegation of corruption is placed against the government – it should make efforts to investigate the claim by the critics rather than rebuke the opposition which it has been doing since the time its government was formed at the centre.

With every passing day the iron curtain of the Sangh Parivar as torch bearer of anti-corruption movement is crumbling making it more & more vulnerable to charges & accusations of opposition parties. Even the hard core supporters of the Sangh Parivar are not convinced about the organization's clean image with regard to corruption and shall soon realize,that it was only a pot calling the kettle black or Devil quoting the scriptures, when the charges of corruption made by Sangh Parivar against UPA-II are revisited. The opposition parties, which have a multitude of issues to pin down the government, are in shambles. The Grand old Party, the Congress which has literally met its nemesis in the 2019 elections with its tally reduced to double digits, seems to have not learnt its lesson even in the hardest way. The Sangh Parivar has shown a lack of temperament and experience in a host of matters concerning national interest and was terribly exposed on not one, but on a number of occasions. The principal opposition parties had never even bothered once to organize a coordinated national campaign to highlight the anti-people policies of the government. In the first instance, the so called secular party should have been immediately on its feet to counter the Sangh Parivar in its attempts to communalize the national polity.

The Grand Old Party on the other hand with its leadership and the president who seem intellectually bankrupt, instead of opposing tooth and nail the Sangh Parivar ideology, has embarked on a pilgrimage to wear the colours of soft Hindutva, to drive home the point that they are Hindus as well. It remains to be seen whether the GOP shall survive in the immediate future, given the amount of lack of wisdom that seems to have piled up at the top. The geo-political scene is fast changing, evolving for the better. Today's Young India is at the cross roads, and in about 5-10 years India will be the youngest country in the world with more that 60 % of the population below the age of 30 years. The young population will be hungry for development of the country and ensure proper utilization of its resources to augment sustained growth. Transformative India going into 2030 through the vision of young India cannot be achieved by the parties such as BJP & the Congress.

While the Sangh Parivar is blatantly using religion to play with the sentiments of the majority for electoral gains, the

Congress party seems to be on its last legs due to an overplay of dynastic politics. Young India should ensure that a diverse, multi-cultural & multi ethnic country is preserved and India becomes truly secular, liberal, tolerant and democracy continues to be the air that we breathe which is consistent with our own vitality. Young India should also realize that religion has no role in Indian politics-whether it is Hindu, Muslim, Christian or Sikh, and any party that misuses religion for its electoral gains should have to be brought down on its knees. Young Indians can be hopeful-since the world over they are being appreciated for entrepreneurship, by launching innovative startups in every enterprise. It would not be long before they devise a successful political idiom that fully ingrains the values & ethos of our constitution. There is no danger to the unity & integrity of our country so long as the evil designs that desperately try to mix religion with politics, to foment a political culture of hate & breed the fever called majoritarianism are slowly cut to size and decimated.

It is also noted with immense concern that the right wing BJP has now returned with a thumping majority in 2019 elections in what could be called as a hugely tampered mandate. It is now even more a challenging task for the secular, liberal Indians to establish a semblance of sanity in the public discourse, as well as return to old cherished values that truly symbolised INDIA

www.ingramcontent.com/pod-product-compliance
Lightning Source LLC
Chambersburg PA
CBHW051230250726

48655CB00006B/2698